The
Yoga
of
Happiness

William James Roberts

Copyright © 2016
William James Roberts
Inner Yoga Media LLC

All rights reserved

ISBN: 0-692-73352-3
ISBN-13: 978-0-692-73352-3

Cover Photograph
Punchbowl Falls in Oregon
© 2012 Lee Rentz, All Rights Reserved

Dedicated

To the real happiness
of all truth seekers.

CONTENTS

1. Soul Living: The Happiness That Lasts 1
2. Who We Really Are 11
3. The Meditative State of Mind 13
4. Meditative Introspection, Positive Change 23
5. The Value of Soul Living 31
Acknowledgements 35
About the Author 37
Praise for The Yoga of Happiness 39

The outer conditions of life will never be
perfect until the inner life is perfect.
The effect cannot precede the cause.

Paramahansa Yogananda

Chapter 1. Soul Living: The Happiness That Lasts

There are many ways to find joy in this world: an achievement or adventure, a good marriage, the birth of a child, a new home, a better job, and so on. But there is only one way to find happiness *and keep it*, and that is to learn who we really are and how to express our true self more in daily life. How can we do it? By using the direct and simple method described in this book.

Ideally we would like to be happy all the time, and it is a little-known fact that with training and self-discipline we can be. I call this book "The Yoga of Happiness" because yoga signifies oneness with our goal as well as a well-defined method for attaining it. And there *is* a sure way to be at one with real happiness.

Practicing The Yoga of Happiness — a way of life that also can be called "soul living" — will develop in us an amazing happiness, deep and abiding even in the midst of trials. This transformation takes place as we go beyond surface notions of who and what we are, and work to develop our deeper nature.

Does that sound appealing? If so, this book is for you.

This chapter presents four essential elements of The Yoga of Happiness: (1) soul understanding, (2) right state of mind, (3) meditative introspection, and (4) right action. The rest of the book explores them further as a way of life that leads to deep fulfillment.

Soul Understanding

The first element of The Yoga of Happiness is a more complete understanding of ourselves. Who we really are is not the same as who we think we are or who we appear to be to others. But then who are we really?

To accept the answer to that question might require a leap of faith, because who we really are is not just the body, not just the mind, but also the soul, a spiritual being that includes mind and body but far transcends their limitations. This fact can be explained in completely nonsectarian terms, and it can be directly experienced in meditation.

As will be explored in Chapters 2-4, the soul for each of us is the "real me". Lasting happiness depends on a willingness to seek out personal experiences of the "real me" and an openness to reworking our ideas and habits based on what we find. Though others' experiences can and should be a guide and an inspiration, ultimately this is something we each must do for ourselves.

So what is the soul really? The soul is not some strange irrelevant thing out there somewhere. It is our very self, operating in multiple dimensions at the same time. It works through body, mind, and spirit all at once, yet its power, vision, and scope are much greater than we know.

For most of us, the soul can operate much more freely through our body and mind than it does now. To the degree that we permit it to do so, it has the power to transform us and benefit everyone around us as well.

The soul, the higher self, sees the things of this world differently. Because it is self-sufficient, the soul has no use for greed or selfishness. It does not seek joy or power by taking from others, because it already has complete joy and fulfillment within itself.

The soul sees — and urges us to affirm — the best in ourselves and in others at all times. It consistently wants the good of all, which goes a long way toward resolving conflicts or actually avoiding them in the first place. That is why the soul, working through us as individuals, can bring much more peace and harmony in the world.

Because the soul is happiness itself, shouldn't we do everything we can to learn more about it?

To do this, we have to at least act as if we believe that such a thing as the soul exists and can be experienced. That is the initial leap of faith mentioned above.

A great way to develop awareness of the soul is to study the lives and writings of one or more spiritual masters — those who have explored the soul most deeply — such as any of the founders of the great world religions.

But the best way I know to accelerate our experience of the soul is to meditate on the breath — a completely non-sectarian activity. Anyone can practice it, religious or not.

Chapter 3 will explain much more about the practice of meditation on the breath, which is key to finding real, lasting happiness.

Right State of Mind

Meditation on the breath lays the foundation for the second element of The Yoga of Happiness: right state of mind.

Breath is the link between our embodied mind and our soul, which is why soul-awareness develops naturally as a by-product of meditating on the breath. This meditative awareness is the right state of mind for practicing The Yoga of Happiness.

As we learn to meditate on the breath, we begin to experience greater peace and intuitive direction. Gradually we assimilate the soul's point of view toward ourselves and our environment, and we learn how to create the conditions for a much happier life.

Meditative Introspection

Meditative introspection, the third element of The Yoga of Happiness, develops naturally as meditation becomes part of our daily life.

What is meditative introspection? It has many aspects, but one of the most amazing is the faculty of perceiving new kinds of meaningful interactions between our thoughts and feelings on the one hand and outer events on the other.

Alert meditators discover for themselves a real, moment-by-moment interaction between outer events and the inner flow of sensations, memories, feelings, desires, thoughts, and plans.

Through the continued practice of meditation, we become aware of the deeper significance of many remarkable coincidences that otherwise would escape us.

The Yoga of Happiness

A Meaningful New Language

In this way, developing intuition teaches us a meaningful new language. As we observe the conscious interplay between what we encounter in the world and what we desire, think, feel, and intend, we learn a whole new language for understanding the meaning of life and our place in it.

It is a language of mutually responsive interactions between our inner and outer worlds, and it opens up ever-increasing avenues for learning. Each external experience potentially reflects on our inner life in its minutest detail, and vice versa.

Meditative introspection also involves asking questions like these: What can I learn from this experience about myself, not just my neighbors and my world? What should my attitude and my behavior be in this situation? How can it help me to bring forth a better version of myself — one more aligned with my soul?

Chapter 4 will shed more light on meditative introspection and how it encourages us to change ourselves so we can "be the change we want to see in the world."

Inner Development: The Basis for Right Action

The first three elements of a truly happy life — soul understanding, right state of mind, and meditative introspection — are ones of inner development.

Practicing the first two elements helps us begin to know ourselves as souls — multi-dimensional beings — as we strive to understand the soul's nature and to develop meditative awareness.

Practicing the third element, meditative introspection, deepens the bond between our inner life and the outer events of the world. As we learn from the increasingly rich interplay between inner experiences and outer events, we gain the insight to change our thoughts and habits for the better.

It is then that we must combine our meditative insights with right action. Doing so empowers and transforms us, converting tentative belief in the soul into a living faith that is anchored in personal experience.

Right action expresses the power of the soul for positive change.

Right Action

Right action is the fourth element of The Yoga of Happiness: the art of conducting ourselves according to the soul's perspective. Right action has two parts: (1) improving ourselves on the inside, and (2) improving the world through soul-directed activity.

The Four Basic Elements of The Yoga of Happiness

The Yoga of Happiness comes down to learning and practicing these four elements:

- First, we strive to understand the nature of the soul, our true multi-dimensional self — that's <u>soul understanding</u>.

- Next, we begin to see things from the soul's point of view, with meditative peace and inner direction — that's <u>right state of mind</u>.

- Third, we learn to explore and be instructed by the conscious interplay between inner awareness and outer events — that's <u>meditative introspection</u>.

- And finally, we try our best to be a force for good by expressing our soul qualities, the very best that is within us, in both our inner life and our outer activity — that's <u>right action</u>.

**The Yoga of Happiness
Develops Deep Fulfillment**

Practiced as a way of life, these four elements form the basis of soul living. I can tell you from my own life and from the lives of many friends and mentors that soul living really works. It brings deep happiness, and the more we practice it the happier we become.

Chapter 2.
Who We Really Are

Not everyone accepts the idea that there is a soul or higher self. We may ask: If we all have a soul, why aren't we all aware of it? Well, at the outset of life we're more or less unaware of it because that is part of the plan.

The higher self exists within each of us much as the plant exists in the seed or the adult inside the child. Every positive action nourishes it, but time and right environment are needed for its full development.

When it comes to the inner life, people really are like plants: they start out in the dark, but sooner or later they grow toward the light. Like seeds in the soil, they eventually move into a life of greater freedom. Some emerge quickly while others, like one species of bamboo, may remain dormant for years, only to sprout all at once and grow to an immense height.

People usually think of the higher self as remote and unattainable, but it isn't. With time and training we can experience it as a living reality here and now. The timing depends on the individual, that's all.

Once we do come to experience the soul moment by moment and day by day, we know for certain that it is real. What is the best way to experience it? By practicing meditation on the breath, a technique presented in the next chapter.

Chapter 3.
The Meditative State of Mind

At some point every truth-seeker turns to meditation. Meditation helps us to become calm and clear enough to see what is true, and to experience the unconditional happiness of the soul.

How we each experience meditation is unique from the outset, because no two people approach or experience truth in exactly the same way. Yet there are several meditation techniques that even experienced meditators will find helpful: progressive relaxation, perception of energy, use of the eye mudra, and meditation on the breath.

Technique of Progressive Relaxation

One of the best preparations for meditation or any other important activity is to relax. Let us now perform a simple exercise in progressive relaxation.

Slowly inhale, and gradually and mindfully tense the entire body as much as you comfortably can. Hold the tension for a few moments. Then exhale as you gradually and mindfully release it.

Repeat the exercise a few more times. It promotes calmness, and it also teaches us to feel the difference between ordinary tension and calm, energized relaxation.

Many people identify energy with tension. They believe that to feel strong they must be mentally tense or nervous, but that is not true. Even though muscular tension results from directing energy to our muscles, the energy itself is superior to and different from the tension that it causes.

Progress in The Yoga of Happiness enables us to consciously feel calm energy and to mindfully exercise calm willpower.

We learn to be strong and quick without being restless and nervous. We learn to be alert and active without excess tension in body or mind: calm when we are at rest, and also calm while we are active. That state of calm empowerment supports excellence in every activity of our lives.

Practicing the Perception of Energy

With all this in mind, please practice the technique of progressive relaxation one more time. Afterwards, can you feel tingling sensations in your body? If you can, what you are feeling is your life force, known to practitioners of yoga or the martial arts as *prana* or *chi*.

It is good to concentrate on this energy regularly, and a great time to do it is right after waking up in the morning.

We also can pause during the day to feel it from time to time, and we can visualize it as a force field all around us – because all living beings do have this electromagnetic field around them, and placing our attention on it can reinforce the field.

Using the Eye Mudra

The eye mudra is something that anyone can do alone or with others. It calms our thoughts, making them more positive, and over time it becomes a real asset in overcoming moods and compulsions.

To perform the eye mudra we shift our attention to the mid-spot between the eyebrows, just above the nose. We can do this whether we are meditating or not. If we are not meditating, we lift our attention only, not our eyes.

How to Use the Eye Mudra During Meditation

- Close your eyes, and slightly lift them as you direct your attention to the mid-spot between the eyebrows. This is a vital point of spiritual perception often referred to as the "spiritual eye."

- Do not lift your eyes to the point of strain!

- While meditating on the breath as explained below, keep your eyes lifted and keep part of your attention at the spiritual eye.

- After meditating on the breath, return your whole focus to the spiritual eye.

- We can train ourselves to keep at least a portion of our attention at the spiritual eye at all times, whether or not our eyes are lifted.

Meditation on the Breath

Meditation on the breath comes in many forms. The technique presented below has been practiced for centuries, and you can get good results just by doing it on your own. Ideally, though, try to find a few like-minded persons and meditate with them regularly as well. This will support your own meditation practice enormously.

Technique of Meditation on the Breath

(Experienced meditators can regard this as a review of the technique. If you already practice a different version of meditation on the breath, it is perfectly all right to continue meditating as before.)

- Find a quiet, comfortable place away from pets and other people (unless those people are meditating with you). A secluded and well-ventilated area is best for regular practice, though really you can use the technique almost anywhere.

- Sit on a chair with feet flat on the floor or, if you prefer, sit cross-legged on the floor or on a firm cushion or mattress. One way or another, keep your body stable, spine straight, and chin level.

- Place your hands, with palms upturned, where your thighs join your abdomen or as close to that position as you can comfortably manage.

- The idea is to sit so comfortably that you won't want to move a muscle. More than almost anything else, sitting motionless helps to calm down the restless mind.

- Whether you are meditating alone or with others, use the eye mudra: Close your eyes, lift them slightly, and direct your attention to the mid-spot between the eyebrows. This also helps to quiet your thoughts and focus your attention.

- When you are meditating in public — for example, in a plane, a park, or a restaurant — it is fine to keep your eyes open.

- If you are religious, lovingly ask the God of your understanding to bless your meditation. Singing, chanting, or praying — either silently or out loud — can deepen your devotion and increase your concentration.

- *Optional*: Do not strain, but gradually tense the whole body as you take a deep breath, then exhale as you gradually relax. Repeat three to six times.

- Now, keeping part of your focus at the spiritual eye, pay careful attention to your breathing. Notice how the breath flows in and flows out. Don't try to control it, just watch it impartially as though you were watching someone else breathe.

The Meditative State of Mind

- Notice any sensations, feelings, memories, or thoughts that arise, but don't dwell on them. Let them come and go freely.

- If your attention does wander, don't be upset. Just refocus on the breath and on the eye mudra. Refocusing is actually a valuable part of meditation.

- Newcomers to meditation may want to start out meditating for 5-10 minutes and gradually work up to longer periods. Particularly at the outset, attentiveness is much more important than duration.

- Do not jump up after you finish concentrating on the breath. Sit still for few moments longer, and pay special attention to even the slightest perception of peace, joy, love, or calmness. By focusing on it, you will increase its power in your life.

- Notice the difference in your perceptions, feelings, thoughts, and determinations after you meditate. Journaling can be very helpful, especially in a spiritual diary that you revisit year after year.

- The period after meditation is an excellent time for problem-solving or any other creative activity.

- It also is the very best time to pray for yourself and others.

At first, meditation on the breath may seem more like a release for pent-up thoughts and feelings than a way to quiet and concentrate the mind. With time and discipline, though, the inner turbulence settles down so that a new and clearer vision can emerge.

The Transforming Power of Meditation

Meditation on the breath appears to be simple but it is transformational because, as I mentioned in Chapter 1, breath is the link between the soul and the embodied mind. So meditation on the breath is an incredibly powerful tool. It develops a spiritually open and discerning state of mind — the right state of mind for cultivating lasting happiness.

Most of us have heard about meditating to reduce stress and improve efficiency, and meditation certainly can do those things. However, meditation on the breath does much more. The regular practice of meditation on the breath can open up a whole new way of life. Why? Because it establishes a widening conduit to our higher self, the soul.

Meditation on the breath also prepares the body and the mind for even more advanced meditation techniques. Dedicated meditators will automatically attract these techniques in due time: "when the student is ready the teacher will appear."

Chapter 4. Meditative Introspection & Positive Change

As we make meditation on the breath part of our daily life, we often notice signs of a new harmony and a new enthusiasm. We may effortlessly find ourselves doing the right things at the right time. We may sense a new rapport with family members, coworkers, or friends. This much is certain: by persevering in meditation we will find life much more fascinating than ever before.

Even beginners in meditation may have life-changing interior experiences, but with dedicated practice everyone will attract great joy, beauty, and power.

Of course the opposite can happen, too. Meditation makes us more self-aware, and sometimes we can't help recognizing behaviors that we need to change. The good news is that meditation also makes us more skillful at appreciating the good in ourselves and better able to initiate positive changes in our lives.

The Mirror of Meditative Introspection

For those who really want truth and happiness, meditative introspection is a mirror that increasingly shows things as they really are. It reveals a new kind of perception. We begin to notice when outer events reflect or answer our own unexpressed thoughts and feelings, and we study this meaningful interplay between what is inside us and what certainly appears to be outside. By doing this, we open the door to an increasing variety of truth perceptions.

Experiences of synchronicity come in time to all truth seekers. Outer events, pleasant or not, are perceived as having distinctly personal meaning and instructive power. Seen in this way, events stimulate us to overcome personal limitations and to learn more about the unconditional love, unfailing understanding, and all-benefiting power that belong to our true nature as souls.

Our Dual Nature in This World

With study, meditation, and meditative introspection, we begin to know deep down who we really are and what our life's purpose really is.

We see that, like everyone else, we have an "ego" or lower self that caters to personal likes and dislikes, but we actually are a "soul," a spiritual being that constantly urges us toward actions that will serve the greater good. The ego or lower self is always about me, me, me, me, me. The soul or higher self is about the real me: the spiritual me that shares in the life and contributes to the happiness of all.

Meditative introspection urges us more and more to identify with the happiness and the all-encompassing vision of the soul, our true self. The more we experience the soul, the more we feel unconditionally guided, inspired, and cherished by that overarching presence.

Setting Goals and Staying Positive

What happens when we gain a better understanding of our life's purpose? We identify habits and conditions that need improvement, and we set about changing them.

For some of us, there could be an initial period of meditative introspection when we become acutely aware of things we've done wrong in the past. This is normal and nothing to be afraid of, because everyone makes mistakes and the important thing is to learn from them and move on.

In addition to acknowledging past errors (and, where appropriate, trying to make amends for them), of course we want to learn from them so we don't repeat them in the future. To do this most effectively, we should work to improve not only our behavior but also our understanding of who we really are.

We are not the erring ego, we are the soul in reality; and all souls are worthy of love and respect. Soul understanding is essential to positive change, as it enables us to develop unconditional love. So the final step in improving our behavior is for us to strive to love ourselves unconditionally as the soul-directed persons we are striving to become.

No matter what difficulties we face, through our daily efforts at soul living we can vanquish them all. Each of us has a different script, a different set of challenges, but our only requirement is to try and give our best each day.

In fact, doing that is the fourth element of The Yoga of Happiness: right action. It is not always easy to express our soul qualities in everyday life, but making the effort is what counts. Effort *is* progress, as a friend once said.

There is a helpful cycle we can use to make steadier progress:

1. Meditate.

2. Think while we are in a state of meditative awareness.

3. Act accordingly.
4. Reflect and think some more.

In this way we can tackle any difficulty and emerge victorious. Repeating this cycle frequently will bring our attitudes, ambitions, and actions into greater alignment with the soul.

Doing the Next Right Thing

With practice at meditation and prayer, we gain a powerful weapon against making harmful choices: our developing intuition.

When we are tempted to make a harmful choice, one that is not true to our higher self — or afterwards if we already have succumbed — there is a very simple way to get back on track. We can just ask ourselves, "What is the next right thing that I should do?"

As soon as intuition reveals the answer, we then do it without hesitation to the very best of our ability. This keeps us in the present moment, which is where we have to be to experience happiness and freedom.

Then we simply repeat this process of asking and doing until we feel strong and happy again. Decisive action, guided by soul intuition, works wonders.

Of course, we cannot achieve happiness and success alone, nor are we meant to. Good company is so important that whole books can be written about the subject — far more than I can touch on here. For purposes of this book I will only say that having at least one or two good friends — those who bring us strength and peace — is vitally important for most of us. Meditating, relaxing, and working together with our true friends makes a huge contribution to our long-term success.

Becoming successful at soul living takes time, training, and sustained effort. Sure, it can be a battle; but the better we get at it, the more each day becomes brand new experience of joy and soul-awareness.

Soul living actually is very simple. We just add regular meditation and introspection to a kind and active life, that's all. The only requirement for this way of life is an open heart and a positive mind regardless of any setbacks.

**How Inner Transformation
Brings Happiness and Success**

The Yoga of Happiness make us stronger and more creative in every way. We become far more aware and watchful of our motives and our intentions, and far more capable of recognizing and replacing harmful thoughts, feelings, and actions with beneficial ones.

The process of meditative introspection and the reward of soul living are vividly described in "Divine Harmony," an essay by Paramahansa Yogananda in the book, *Journey to Self-Realization*:

> The mind is nature's incinerator wherein you can burn to ashes all mental dross that is not worthy to be saved: your waste thoughts and desires, your misconceptions and grievances, and your discords in human relationships. There is not a single relationship, however estranged, you cannot reconcile, provided you do so first in your own mind. There is not a single problem in life you cannot resolve, provided you first solve it in your inner world, its place of origin. Be not intimidated by consequences, even though they be drastic. Before you act, if you first harmonize the situation with the discriminative wisdom in your mind, the outcome will take care of itself. A harmonized mind produces harmony in this world of seeming discord.

The Yoga of Happiness

Soul living bestows the power to harmonize our mind, and perseverance in harmonious living infallibly brings all-around success.

Chapter 5.
The Value of Soul Living

Soul living also draws amazing friends into our lives. As Ralph Waldo Emerson said, true "friendship, like the immortality of the soul, is too good to be believed." One of my mentors once remarked that we have to "reprogram our minds" to accept the deeper truths of this way of life.

Deep happiness invariably comes to everyone who makes a persistent effort at The Yoga of Happiness. The right friends, the right work, a love of meditative peace and joy — these are some of the sure signs of progress in soul living.

The more we practice The Yoga of Happiness, the more we see that real, lasting happiness comes from inner freedom and meditative training to know and to do what is right. It comes from daily practice at finding joy within and discovering the best in everyone and everything.

As we begin to find that indescribable joy, we gradually stop doing what most people do in this world — we stop seeking happiness by trying to control others. We learn that our own greatest benefit (as well as theirs) comes from finding and expressing the freedom to be unconditionally happy. The opportunity to seek and to express that happiness is the most meaningful freedom of all.

Experiences of ecstatic peace and joy await us all as we learn to live centered in the soul. We find ourselves transformed in a most encouraging way. We realize that we are constantly in the supportive presence of our soul, the great dynamo of all our strength, love, and wisdom. We realize that we are never alone.

Learning to "Look at Life Unmasked"

Soul living is the process of learning to see things clearly and to do the right things at the right time. The vital importance of always trying to make choices conducive to our true happiness becomes clear from this final quotation by Yogananda, the author of *Autobiography of a Yogi* and subject of the movie *Awake*:

> There are only two ways to travel in life: one leads to happiness and the other to sorrow. There is no mystery about life; it is very simple in spite of its apparent complexities. You should look at life unmasked, in the mirror of your experiences. View time and space as they come to you in the form

of problems, experiences, and relations. Look at the perpetual current of emotions and thoughts that arise within you. Go into the heart of your aspirations, dreams, hopes, and despairs. Dive deep into the mute cravings of your inner self. Life is manifesting itself through all these channels and demanding that you seek understanding with your highest intelligence, wisdom, love, and vision.

I hope the information in this little book will help you to choose, more and more consistently, the way that leads to the true and incomparable happiness of the soul.

The Yoga of Happiness

Acknowledgements

I want to thank my wife Cathy first and foremost. This book never would have materialized without her wonderful presence in my life.

I am also very grateful to the following friends for their careful reading and constructive criticism: Bryan Born, Nancy Lawlor, Liz Marabeas, Ellyn McNamara, Deborah Myers, Marty Rather, and Tineke Wilders.

The Yoga of Happiness

About the Author

The author lives in the Greater Detroit area and may be reached at WJR.Author@gmail.com. (Note the period after 'WJR'.)

Praise for The Yoga of Happiness

"This is a beautifully written book. Simple, honest, easy to follow instructions that inspire soul searching. I can sense the author's lightness of spirit and depth of soul. Thank you for sharing your light in *The Yoga of Happiness*, William James Roberts."
– Gabriele H.

"I just finished reading your inspiring book! I love the 'technique of meditation on the breath' — I practiced it after reading each step, and it works! Good reminder for meditators and those just beginning. This book will be a faithful companion to whoever reads it. I found it full of hope and positivity, encouraging the reader to take a journey to rediscover their soul, helping themselves and others along the way. I found myself more 'present' after reading the book and in a calm, peaceful place."
– Cathy R.

"I just read your book. It made me tear up, pointing to answers to some questions I have had in my journey.

"You write so eloquently, making sense out of what seemed complex. I absolutely loved your book. I believe it will help many people. It helped me.

"I felt connected as I read each paragraph. I felt as though I understood. I feel my soul peering out of the eyes of this body. I feel a separate entity watching what I do, evaluating, guiding, connecting at times. I have a sense of awareness of that soul living in me. ... Understanding the unknown a little. Grasping a thread of that knowledge.

"This is a beautiful, enlightening book. It helped me see light and a better way to focus, accept goodness, and concentrate on being kind — the way God would like us to be. I am so much happier when I help someone. I do understand, a little better, that trying is what is important, or getting back up every time we fall down. Your book made that known and understandable. You are truly gifted. Your words are truth."

– Laura H.

"This is a spiritual jewel: a great little book packed with spiritual power. I highly recommend you buy it for yourself and gift it to others. It's an easy read and very practical."

– **Ellyn M.**

Made in the USA
Middletown, DE
16 November 2018